Saturn

Uranus

Neptune

Mercury and Venus

Editor in chief: Paul A. Kobasa
Supplementary Publications: Jeff De La Rosa, Lisa Kwon,
    Christine Sullivan, Scott Thomas, Marty Zwikel
Research: Mike Barr, Cheryl Graham, Jacqueline Jasek
    Barbara Lightner, Andy Roberts,
Graphics and Design: Kathy
    Charlene Epple, Tom Eva
Permissions: Janet Peterson
Indexing: David Pofelski
Pre-Press and Manufacturing: Carma Fazio, Anne Fritzinger,
    Steven Hueppchen, Tina Ramirez
Writer: Al Smuskiewicz

First edition published 2006. Second edition published 2007.

WORLD BOOK and the GLOBE DEVICE are registered
trademarks or trademarks of World Book, Inc.

World Book, Inc.
233 N. Michigan Avenue
Chicago, IL 60601
U.S.A.

Library of Congress Cataloging-in-Publication Data
Mercury and Venus. -- 2nd ed.
    p. cm. -- (World Book's solar system & space exploration
brary)
    Summary: "Introduction to Mercury and Venus, providing to
    rimary and intermediate grade students information on their
    features and exploration. Includes fun facts, glossary, resource
list and index" -- Provided by publisher.
    Includes bibliographical references and index.
    ISBN-13: 978-0-7166-9517-2
    ISBN-10: 0-7166-9517-0
    1. Mercury (Planet)--Juvenile literature. 2. Venus (Planet)--
Juvenile literature.   I. World Book, Inc.
    QB611.M472 2007
    523.41--dc22
                                    2006030043

ISBN-13 (set): 978-0-7166-9511-0
ISBN-10 (set): 0-7166-9511-1

Printed in the United States of America

1 2 3 4 5 6 7 8 09 08 07 06

**For information about other World Book publications,
visit our Web site at http://www.worldbook.com or call
1-800-WORLDBK (967-5325).**

**For information about sales to schools and libraries,
call 1-800-975-3250 (United States);
1-800-837-5365 (Canada).**

Picture Acknowledgments: Back Cover: NASA; NASA/JPL; NASA; NASA; Inside Back Cover: © John
Gleason, Celestial Images.

Mercury Attaching his Winged Sandals (1744), marble sculpture by Jean-Baptiste Pigalle, Louvre, Paris
(Bridgeman Art Library) 25; *Venus Crouching* (1686), marble sculpture by Antoine Coysevox, Louvre, Paris
(Bridgeman Art Library) 55; © Calvin J. Hamilton 13, 39; Lunar and Planetary Institute 51; NASA 15, 23,
29, 31, 41, 59, 61; NASA/JPL 43, 49, 53; © Chris Butler, SPL/Photo Researchers 37; © John Chumack,
Photo Researchers 17; © David A. Hardy, Photo Researchers 11; © Frank Zullo, Photo Researchers 27, 57.

Illustrations: Inside Front Cover: WORLD BOOK illustration by Steve Karp; Front Cover & 1, 3, 9, 21, 35,
47: WORLD BOOK illustrations by Paul Perreault; WORLD BOOK illustrations by Precision Graphics 7, 33.

Astronomers use different kinds of photos to learn about objects in space—such as planets. Many photos
show an object's natural color. Other photos use false colors. Some false-color images show types of light
the human eye cannot normally see. Others have colors that were changed to highlight important features.
When appropriate, the captions in this book state whether a photo uses natural or false color.

WORLD BOOK'S

SOLAR SYSTEM & SPACE EXPLORATION LIBRARY

Mercury and Venus

SECOND EDITION

World Book, Inc.
a Scott Fetzer company
Chicago

Contents

MERCURY

If a word is printed in **bold letters that look like this,** that word's meaning is given in the glossary on page 63.

VENUS

Where Is Mercury?

Mercury is the **planet** closest to the sun in our **solar system.** Mercury's **orbit** is between the sun and the orbit of Venus.

Mercury is the nearest to the sun of those planets **astronomers** call the inner planets. The other inner planets are Venus, Earth, and Mars.

The average distance of Earth from the sun is about three times greater than Mercury's average distance from the sun. Mercury and Earth orbit the sun in **elliptical** paths. Sometimes these paths bring the two planets as close together as about 48 million miles (77.3 million kilometers). Other times, the paths carry the planets as far away from each other as about 138 million miles (222 million kilometers).

Mercury's distance from the sun and from its nearest neighbor, Venus, varies over time. On average, Mercury is about 36 million miles (58 million kilometers) from the sun. On average, the planet is about 31 million miles (50 million kilometers) closer to the sun than Venus is.

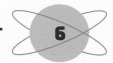

Planet Locator

Note: The size of the sun and planets and the distance between planets in this diagram are not to scale.

Sun

Mercury

Venus

Earth

Mars

Jupiter

Saturn

Uranus

Neptune

Mercury's symbol (top left) and a diagram showing the planet's location in the solar system

How Big Is Mercury?

Mercury is the smallest of the eight **planets** in our **solar system.** Mercury is even smaller than Saturn's **moon** Titan *(TY tuhn)* or Jupiter's moon Ganymede *(GAN uh meed).* At its **equator,** Mercury has a **diameter** of 3,032 miles (4,879 kilometers).

Earth's moon, which is 2,159 miles (3,474 kilometers) in diameter, is a little smaller than Mercury. But, Mercury is less than half the size of Earth.

Mercury's small size is one reason it is hard to see from Earth. Mercury usually appears as a tiny dot of light in the sky when the planet is seen from Earth's surface.

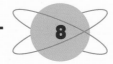

An artist's drawing comparing the size of Mercury and Earth

Mercury's diameter
3,032 miles (4,879 kilometers)

Earth's diameter
7,926 miles (12,756 kilometers)

What Does Mercury Look Like?

Mercury appears to be a tiny point of light when seen from Earth's surface. From a closer distance, Mercury looks like a small, rocky world covered with many round **craters.** These craters were formed when large **meteorites** crashed into the **planet** long ago.

When seen through a telescope, Mercury seems to change in shape and size—much like Earth's **moon** appears to change from night to night as it goes through its **phases.** The change in how Mercury looks happens because different parts of Mercury's sunlit side can be seen at different times. Sometimes only a sliver of the sunlit side can be seen from Earth (as our moon looks to us when it is in a crescent phase). At other times, the entire sunlit side can be seen (as our moon looks to us when it is a full moon). For both Mercury and the moon, there are many phases between the crescent and full phases.

An artist's drawing of Mercury (left) and the sun

What Makes Up Mercury?

Mercury is mostly a big ball of **iron.** It has a thin layer of **minerals** on its surface. This is called the **crust.** Underneath the crust is a thin, rocky layer called the **mantle.** The mantle may be hot enough to have partly molten (melted) rocks, but scientists are not sure about this.

Beneath the mantle, in the center of the **planet,** is a large iron **core.** Mercury's core takes up much more of the inside of Mercury than does Earth's core. Some scientists think that the outer part of Mercury's core may be filled with flowing hot, molten iron.

Such deep, flowing iron would conduct electricity. This would explain why Mercury has a **magnetic field.** The Mariner 10 space **probe,** launched by the United States National Aeronautics and Space Administration (NASA) in 1973, first detected Mercury's magnetic field. This field bends the paths of electrically charged particles coming from the sun.

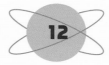

The Interior of Mercury

Crust of minerals

Rocky mantle

Mostly iron core

What Is Mercury's Atmosphere Like?

The Mariner 10 space **probe** found that Mercury is almost airless, like Earth's **moon.** The **planet** has only a very thin **atmosphere,** made up mostly of **sodium** vapor and **helium** and **hydrogen** gas. There is also a tiny bit of **oxygen** in the atmosphere—but not nearly enough to allow an animal to breathe. Thicker patches of air form every now and then, but they quickly disappear.

Some scientists think that Mercury may have had a thicker atmosphere billions of years ago. One possible reason for the thinning of Mercury's atmosphere could have been the planet's small size. Because it is so small, Mercury has only a weak force of **gravity.** Mercury's gravity may not have been strong enough to hold onto its early atmosphere. That would have allowed the chemicals of the atmosphere to scatter into space.

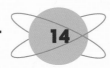

Mercury in a black-and-white photo

What Is the Weather on Mercury?

The weather on Mercury is known for its extreme temperatures. Mercury is both very hot and very cold!

Because Mercury is so close to the sun, the solar rays that reach the **planet** are about seven times stronger than the rays that reach Earth. This makes daytime (that is, the time when a region of Mercury is facing the sun) very hot. The temperature on Mercury for a region facing the sun can reach 840 °F (450 °C).

Although daytime on Mercury is hot, nighttime (the time when a region of Mercury is facing away from the sun) is very cold. The planet's nighttime temperature can drop to as low as −275 °F (−170 °C). The reason it gets so cold at night is because the atmosphere is too thin to trap the heat from the day. So, the heat escapes into space as soon as the sun sets.

It is also very dry on Mercury, with no rain or snow. There are never any clouds in Mercury's sky. The sky is always perfectly clear, and it is as black as it is at nighttime on Earth—even during daytime on Mercury.

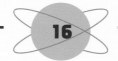

Mercury crosses in front of the sun in this photo made through a telescope

Mercury

Sun

How Does Mercury Compare with Earth?

Mercury's **mass** is much smaller than the mass of Earth. But Mercury's **density** is only a little less than the density of Earth. So, a chunk of Mercury would weigh just slightly less than an equal-sized chunk of Earth.

Mercury's **gravity** is only about one-third as strong as Earth's gravity. That is because Mercury is less massive—or contains less matter—than does Earth. Because weight depends on gravity, you would weigh less on Mercury than you do on Earth. If you weighed 100 pounds on Earth, you would weigh only about 38 pounds on Mercury.

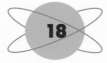

How Do They Compare?

	Earth ⊕	Mercury ☿
Size in diameter (at equator)	7,926 miles (12,756 kilometers)	3,032 miles (4,879 kilometers)
Average distance from sun	About 93 million miles (150 million kilometers)	About 36 million miles (58 million kilometers)
Length of year (in Earth days)	365.256	87.969
Length of day (in Earth time)	24 hours	176 Earth days (although, Mercury rotates on its axis once every 59 Earth days)
What an object would weigh...	If it weighed 100 pounds on Earth...	...it would weigh about 38 pounds on Mercury.
Number of moons	1	0
Rings?	No	No
Atmosphere	Nitrogen, oxygen, argon	Sodium, helium, hydrogen, oxygen

What Are the Orbit and Rotation of Mercury Like?

Mercury rotates (spins around) very slowly on its **axis.** But the **planet** also **orbits** very quickly around the sun. This leads to something unusual about Mercury. The length of Mercury's **day** is twice as long as its **year!**

The path of Mercury's orbit is **elliptical.** Sometimes Mercury is as close as about 28.5 million miles (46 million kilometers) to the sun. Other times it is as far away from the sun as about 43 million miles (70 million kilometers). Mercury's average distance from the sun is about 36 million miles (58 million kilometers).

The speed at which Mercury orbits the sun is very fast. The sun's **gravity** pulls Mercury around the sun faster than any other planet in the **solar system.** Mercury races around the sun at about 30 miles (48 kilometers) per second. It orbits the sun about once every 88 Earth days—that is the length of one Mercury year.

Mercury takes 59 Earth days to rotate once on its axis. During that rotation, however, it completes ⅔ of its orbit around the sun. So, if you count a day on Mercury as being from sunrise to sunrise, the length of a day on Mercury is 176 Earth days long.

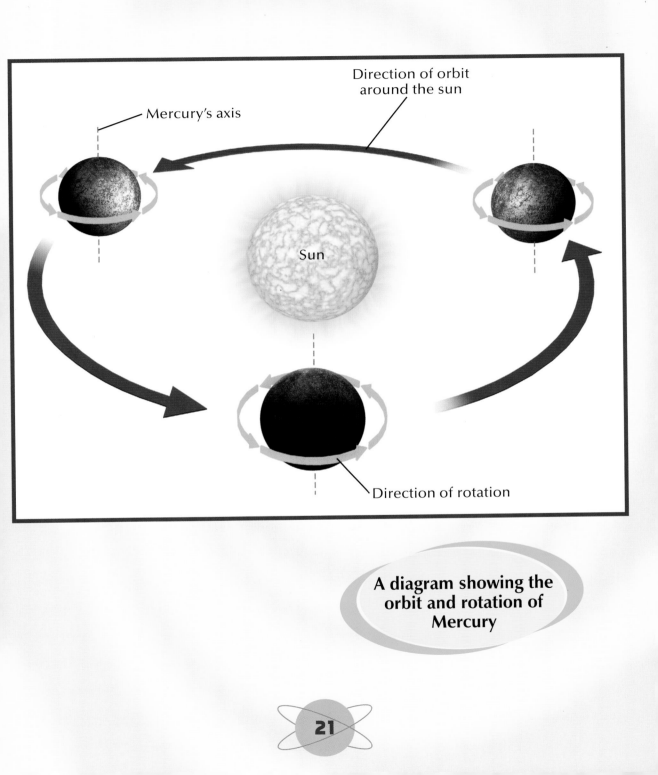

Direction of orbit
around the sun

Mercury's axis

Sun

Direction of rotation

A diagram showing the
orbit and rotation of
Mercury

What Is the Surface of Mercury Like?

NASA's Mariner 10 space **probe** photographed about half of Mercury's surface. The photos showed many deep **craters** dotting flat areas. The largest crater on Mercury is Caloris Basin, which covers more than one-fourth of the **diameter** of the **planet.** Caloris Basin is about 800 miles (1,300 kilometers) wide—hundreds of miles wider than the largest craters on Earth. The NASA photos also showed long chains of mountains on Mercury.

Mercury's surface also has many long cliffs. Scientists think these cliffs formed billions of years ago. At that time, the planet may have cooled and its shape changed, with its outer **crust** shrinking and buckling.

Mercury also has large, flat plains that may have been caused by erupting volcanoes. Scientists think that about 3 billion years ago, Mercury's volcanoes stopped erupting. Most other activity below the planet's surface stopped too. Scientists doubt that there has been much change to the surface of Mercury since that time.

Caloris Basin in a black-and-white photomosaic

How Did Mercury Get Its Name?

Thousands of years ago, people noticed a "star" that always seemed to follow the sun in the sky. The object could be seen low in the sky just before sunrise and again just after sunset. Some people thought the object they saw in the morning and the one they saw in the evening were two different objects. Eventually, the ancient Greeks realized that these two "stars" were actually a single **planet.**

This planet seemed to move across the sky so quickly from one night to the next that the Romans named it after their speedy, winged messenger of the gods—Mercury. In myths (certain types of legends or stories), Mercury wore winged sandals and a winged hat to help him fly fast.

The planet's symbol (see the illustration on page 7) represents the head of Mercury wearing a winged hat.

A statue of the Roman god Mercury

Where Is Mercury in Earth's Sky?

It is not easy to see Mercury. Mercury is always near the sun, so it often gets lost in the twilight glow of sunset or in the light of sunrise.

When the sky is clear, look for what appears to be a medium-bright star low in the west just after sunset or low in the east just before sunrise. (If you see what appears to be a very bright star in these parts of the sky, however, that is probably Venus.) Mercury is in the west when it is moving toward Earth. It is in the east when moving away from Earth. When Mercury is on the opposite side of the sun from Earth, it cannot be seen.

It's best to use a telescope to look at Mercury. You will then be able to see the **planet** change its shape from day to day as it goes through different **phases.**

Mercury

Mercury in the sky
at sunrise

What Space Missions Have Studied Mercury?

Compared with Venus and Mars, Mercury has not been studied by many space missions. In fact, as of 2005, only one mission—Mariner—had reached the closest **planet** to the sun.

NASA's Mariner 10 flew past Mercury in 1974 and 1975. A camera on the robotic space **probe** photographed about half of Mercury's surface. Another instrument on Mariner 10 measured the planet's **magnetic field.**

Mariner 10 taught NASA scientists a lot about Mercury. But it also helped scientists learn how to design even better space probes to send to the other planets.

In 2004, NASA launched a space probe named Messenger. This probe was scheduled to reach Mercury in 2008. After that, it will fly by the planet a couple of times before orbiting around the planet for a year starting in 2011. The probe will carry out many tasks, including mapping Mercury's surface in greater detail and studying its magnetic field.

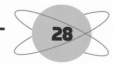

Could There Be Life on Mercury?

Mercury is one of the most uninviting **planets** in the **solar system.** The scorching daytime temperatures on Mercury would likely make it impossible for life to survive on the planet.

In addition, Mercury's thin **atmosphere** is not the kind most life forms we know about can tolerate. As far as we know, life forms cannot really develop in a **vacuum,** and Mercury's atmosphere comes close to being empty space. Further, the thin atmosphere of Mercury allows dangerous solar rays to stream through the air to Mercury's surface. These rays would quickly kill most living organisms on the surface.

Craters on the surface of Mercury in a black-and-white photo

Where Is Venus?

Venus is the second **planet** from the sun. Venus's **orbit** is between the orbits of Earth and Mercury. Venus's orbit lies closer to Earth's orbit than does that of any other planet.

Venus is one of the planets that **astronomers** call the inner planets. The other inner planets are Mercury, Earth, and Mars.

About every 19 months, the nearly circular path of Venus's orbit around the sun brings Venus close to Earth. At their closest, the two planets are almost 24 million miles (38 million kilometers) apart. But, because they travel different paths around the sun, Venus and Earth sometimes move as far away from each other as about 162 million miles (260 million kilometers).

On average, the orbit of Venus is about 67 million miles (108 million kilometers) from the sun. That is about 26 million miles (42 million kilometers) closer to the sun than Earth's orbit is. But, Venus's orbit is about 31 million miles (50 million kilometers) farther out than Mercury's is.

Planet Locator

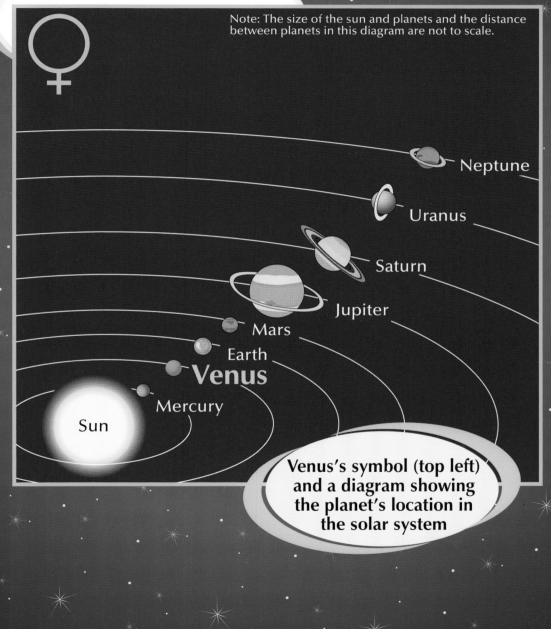

Note: The size of the sun and planets and the distance between planets in this diagram are not to scale.

Neptune

Uranus

Saturn

Jupiter

Mars

Earth

Venus

Mercury

Sun

Venus's symbol (top left) and a diagram showing the planet's location in the solar system

How Big Is Venus?

Venus has sometimes been called "Earth's twin" because both **planets** are about the same size. Venus is 7,521 miles (12,104 kilometers) in **diameter** at the **equator**—only about 400 miles (644 kilometers) smaller than the diameter of Earth.

Venus and Earth are the largest of the four rocky, inner planets that **orbit** near the sun. But, Venus and Earth are small when compared to such outer **gas giants** as Jupiter and Saturn. The diameter of Saturn, for example, is about 10 times as large as the diameter of Venus.

An artist's drawing comparing the size of Venus and Earth

Venus's diameter
7,521 miles (12,104 kilometers)

Earth's diameter
7,926 miles (12,756 kilometers)

What Does Venus Look Like?

From Earth, Venus is brighter than any other **planet** or star in the sky. Venus—like Earth's **moon** and Mercury—appears to change in shape from day to day as it goes through **phases.** The phases of Venus range from a thin sliver to a "full-moon" shape. This happens because different parts of Venus's sunlit side are visible from Earth at different times.

Venus is completely covered in thick and swirling yellowish clouds. So, Venus appears as a bright, yellowish object. The blanket of clouds makes it impossible to see the surface of Venus through a telescope on Earth.

Venus's surface was mostly unknown until space **probes** from the United States and Russia (when it was part of a country called the Soviet Union) visited the planet. Some of these probes landed on Venus's surface and photographed it. Venus's surface was shown to have volcanoes, mountains, and large flat plains.

An artist's drawing
showing clouds on Venus

What Makes Up Venus?

The inside of Venus is probably much like the inside of Earth. Scientists think that underneath the rocky, solid **crust,** there may be a rocky, partly molten (melted) **mantle.** Beneath the mantle, Venus has a **core** that is most likely made up of **iron.** This iron core may be molten (completely liquid and flowing), partially molten, or completely solid. Some scientists think that Venus has a molten-iron outer core and a solid-iron inner core.

The flow of liquid metals in Earth's outer core causes Earth to be surrounded by a **magnetic field,** a field in space that acts like a giant bar magnet. If Venus also has a flowing metal outer core, it would seem that it should also have a magnetic field. Scientists are not sure why, but space **probes** have found no magnetic field around Venus. Many scientists think that something in Venus's core must make it different than Earth's core.

The Interior of Venus

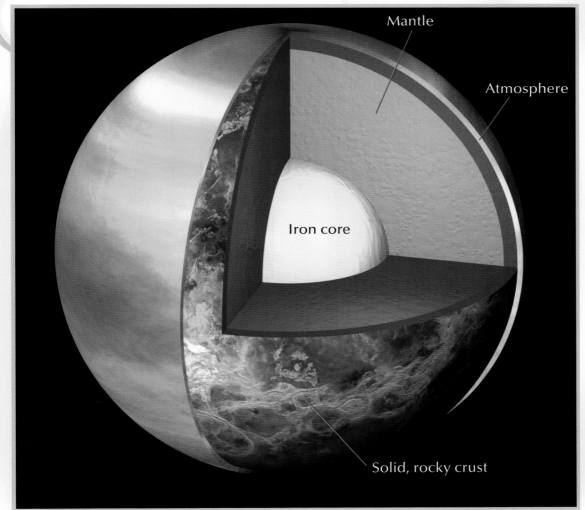

Mantle

Atmosphere

Iron core

Solid, rocky crust

What Is Venus's Atmosphere Like?

The **atmosphere** of Venus is made up mostly of a gas called **carbon dioxide.** The atmosphere also contains small amounts of **nitrogen, argon,** and other substances.

The atmosphere around Venus is very different from the atmosphere around Earth. The Venusian atmosphere is very thick, soupy, and heavy. The weight of the atmosphere bears down on Venus's surface with a **pressure** equal to the pressure of water on Earth at about 2,950 feet (900 meters) below the surface of the ocean.

At least three layers of thick clouds float in the gases of Venus's atmosphere. These clouds are made of droplets of **sulfuric acid,** the same kind of acid used in car batteries. Sulfuric acid is so strong that it is used to dissolve metals. It can burn the skin if touched and damage the lungs if breathed in. Some scientists think these clouds formed on Venus from chemicals released by volcanoes on that planet.

Venus's clouds in an ultraviolet image

What Is the Weather on Venus?

The weather on Venus is very hot. Venus is even hotter than the weather on Mercury. That is because the thick **atmosphere** of Venus traps heat near the surface—much like a greenhouse traps heat to warm plants on Earth. Temperatures during a typical **day** on Venus reach about 870 °F (465 °C).

It is too hot for water to exist on Venus. But observations by NASA space **probes** have led scientists to think that "rain drops"—made of **sulfuric acid**—fall within Venus's clouds. Heat causes these drops to evaporate before they reach the surface of the **planet.**

Winds often blow at speeds of more than 200 miles (320 kilometers) per hour at the cloud tops of Venus. That is about the speed of strong hurricane winds on Earth. Winds at Venus's surface reach only about the speed of a person walking slowly.

Space probe images suggest that lightning may be common on Venus. But scientists are not sure about this.

A series of
photomosaics showing
the clouds that surround
Venus

How Does Venus Compare with Earth?

Venus and Earth are alike in a few ways. Besides being about the same size, the two **planets** have about the same **mass** and **gravity.** So your weight would be close to the same on both planets. If you weighed 100 pounds on Earth, you would weigh about 88 pounds on Venus.

However, space **probes** have shown that, in most ways, Venus is very different from Earth. In fact, Venus's dry surface, soupy **atmosphere,** and superhot weather are extremely different from conditions on Earth.

Scientists believe that about 4 billion years ago Venus was much more like Earth. Then the sun was less bright and not as hot as it is today. At that time, Venus could have had mild temperatures, flowing water, and even an ocean. But, as the sun got brighter and hotter over time, Venus also got hotter and more and more unlike Earth.

How Do They Compare?

	Earth ⊕	Venus ♀
Size in diameter (at equator)	7,926 miles (12,756 kilometers)	7,521 miles (12,104 kilometers)
Average distance from sun	About 93 million miles (150 million kilometers)	About 67 million miles (108 million kilometers)
Length of year (in Earth days)	365.256	224.7
Length of day (in Earth time)	24 hours	243 Earth days
What an object would weigh...	If it weighed 100 pounds on Earth...	...it would weigh about 88 pounds on Venus.
Number of moons	1	0
Rings?	No	No
Atmosphere	Nitrogen, oxygen, argon	Carbon dioxide, nitrogen, water vapor, argon, carbon monoxide, neon, sulfur dioxide

What Are the Orbit and Rotation of Venus Like?

Venus is the only **planet** that **orbits** the sun in an almost perfectly circular path. All the other planets move around the sun in **elliptical** orbits. Venus's orbit keeps it roughly 67 million miles (108 million kilometers) away from the sun.

Venus moves around the sun at about 22 miles (35 kilometers) per second, and it takes the planet 224.7 Earth days to orbit the sun one time. That is the length of one **year** on Venus.

Venus rotates on its **axis** more slowly than any other planet—once every 243 Earth days. That is the length of a single **day** on Venus. So, the length of a day on Venus is longer than the length of that planet's year! Unlike most other planets, Venus actually rotates in the opposite direction from that which it moves around the sun.

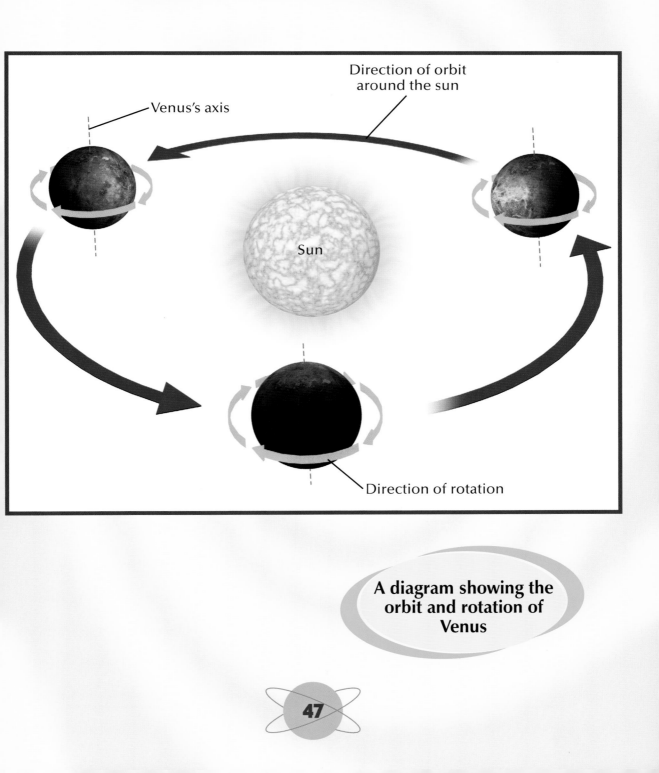

Direction of orbit
around the sun

Venus's axis

Sun

Direction of rotation

A diagram showing the
orbit and rotation of
Venus

What Is the Surface of Venus Like?

Venus is a rocky **planet,** so you could stand on the surface of Venus. But, the planet's thick **atmosphere** makes it hard for scientists to learn about its surface.

Venus has some of the most amazing features in the **solar system.** There are thousands of volcanoes of different sizes—some of them are as wide as 150 miles (240 kilometers). The planet's flat plains are covered with cracked, hardened lava. The lava erupted from volcanoes long ago and later cooled and dried. Venus has no water on its surface. But NASA's Magellan spacecraft, which has been orbiting Venus since 1990, found long, winding "rivers" of hardened lava.

Venus also has high mountains, deep **craters,** and certain unusual features not found on Earth. Among these strange features are coronae *(kuh ROH nee),* or crowns. These large, ringlike structures are as much as 360 miles (580 kilometers) across. On Venus, tesserae *(TEHS uh ree)* are raised areas in which many ridges and valleys formed in different directions. Both coronae and tesserae are evidence of how some regions of the surface of Venus moved and changed over time.

Craters on the surface of Venus in a false-color photo

Does Venus Have Continents?

On Earth, the continents are high areas of land. These continents are surrounded or nearly surrounded by lower areas that contain water—oceans or seas. Venus has two high areas that are like continents. But there is no water around them. These areas are called Aphrodite Terra (*AF ruh DY tee TEHR uh*) and Ishtar Terra (*ISH tahr TEHR uh*).

Aphrodite Terra follows along the **equator** of Venus. There are many volcanoes on Aphrodite Terra. One of the highest of these is Maat Mons, which rises 5 miles (8 kilometers) above the surface of Venus. Aphrodite Terra covers an area about the size of South America.

Ishtar Terra, which is near Venus's north pole, covers an area about the size of Australia. Ishtar Terra has four large mountain ranges, including the Maxwell Montes, which has the highest elevation on Venus. The highest point of the Maxwell Montes rises about 7 miles (11.3 kilometers) into the sky. That is more than 1 mile (1.6 kilometers) higher than Mount Everest, the highest place on Earth.

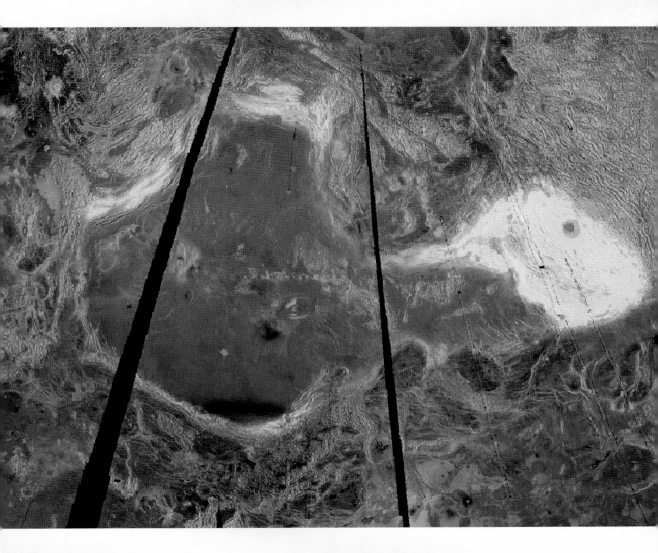

Ishtar Terra in a black-and-white image

Does Venus Have Active Volcanoes?

Volcanic eruptions are one of the main forces that cause change on Earth's surface. The hot lava that erupts from volcanoes flows over the land and covers up older features—almost the way an old road is repaved with asphalt.

Much of the surface of Venus is also "paved" with flows of lava. Most of these flows probably came from volcanoes that erupted more than 500 million years ago. The lava covered up many older **craters.** That is one reason why there are far fewer craters on Venus's surface today than there are on Mercury or Earth's **moon.**

Do volcanoes still erupt on Venus? Scientists are not sure, but some scientists think that there are volcanoes on Venus that may be active from time to time. NASA space **probes** have found possible "hot spots" on the surface that may be signs of hot volcanic vents. Vents are the openings that lava comes out of. Space probes have also found certain gases in the atmosphere that may have been blown out by volcanoes.

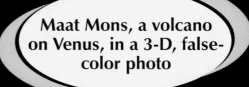

Maat Mons, a volcano on Venus, in a 3-D, false-color photo

How Did Venus Get Its Name?

Thousands of years ago, many people thought Venus was two different **planets.** Later, people realized that the bright object seen in the eastern sky at sunrise and the bright object seen in the western sky at sunset were the same single planet.

The dazzling brightness of Venus led people in ancient China to name it Tai-pe, which means "beautiful white one." The ancient Greeks and Romans linked the planet with mythological goddesses. The Romans named it Venus after their goddess of love and beauty.

Venus is the only planet that the Romans named after a female figure. In addition, almost all **craters,** mountains, and other features on Venus are named after real women, mythological women, or goddesses. Appropriately, the astronomical symbol for Venus (see the illustration on page 33) is the symbol for "woman."

The only feature on Venus named for a man is the mountain range Maxwell Montes—named for the Scottish scientist James Clerk Maxwell (1831–1879).

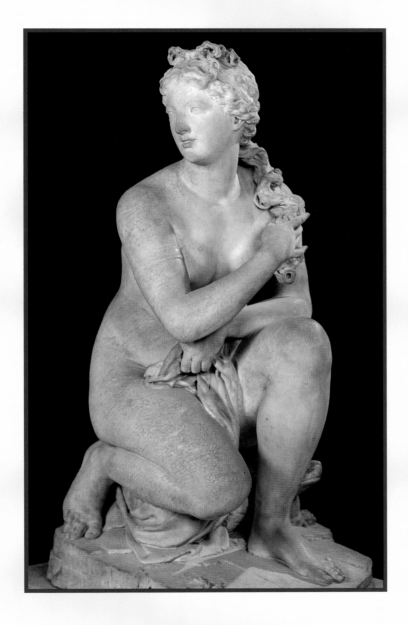

A statue of the Roman goddess Venus

Where Is Venus in Earth's Sky?

Venus is the easiest **planet** to find in the sky, because it is the brightest. Look for what appears to be a very bright star low in the western sky just after sunset, or low in the eastern sky just before sunrise. When Venus is moving toward Earth, it is in the west. When it is moving away from Earth, it is in the east. When Venus is on the other side of the sun from Earth, it cannot be seen.

If you use a telescope to look at Venus, you will be able to see the planet appear to change its shape. From night to night, it will go through different **phases,** as does Earth's moon. You can keep a notebook of your observations and draw sketches of the changing phases of Venus.

Venus and a crescent
moon in the western sky
at sunset

What Space Missions Have Studied Venus?

Much of what we know about Venus has come from missions involving space **probes** that the United States or the former Soviet Union sent to the planet. The Soviet Union launched several Venera spacecraft to either fly by or land on Venus in the 1960's, 1970's, and 1980's. The Venera landers took photographs of the surface and made other observations. Some of these spacecraft lasted as long as 110 minutes before the intense temperatures and crushing **pressures** on Venus destroyed them.

In 1978, the NASA probes Pioneer Venus 1 and Pioneer Venus 2 reached Venus. Pioneer Venus 1 orbited the planet for nearly 14 years, mapping the surface and studying the **atmosphere.** Pioneer Venus 2 dropped special instruments into the atmosphere that measured such things as temperatures and wind speeds.

In the 1990's, NASA's Magellan spacecraft made many detailed pictures of Venus's surface. In 2005, the European Space Agency (ESA) launched the Venus Express probe, which began orbiting Venus in 2006. The probe was designed to study the atmosphere of Venus and to search for signs of ongoing volcanic activity.

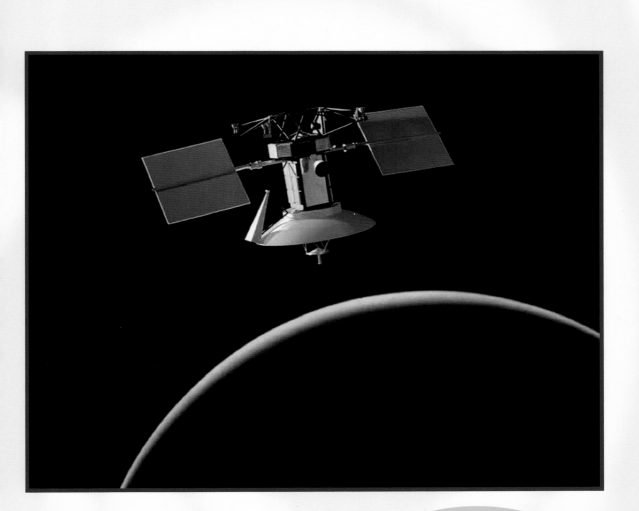

An artist's drawing of the
Magellan spacecraft,
above Venus

Could There Be Life on Venus?

As Venus is today—a waterless world with the highest temperatures in the **solar system**—it could not, according to scientists, support any form of life known on Earth. Although people may one day visit Mars and perhaps even live there for long periods, setting up colonies for humans on Venus is just not possible. The great heat and pressure would instantly kill the visiting astronauts.

Before scientists learned what Mars is really like, many people imagined it to be a place thriving with "little green men" or other forms of life. As recently as 50 years ago, people had similar ideas about Venus. Because Venus is so close to the sun, some people thought that it might be a warm, swampy paradise, like some tropical places on Earth. They imagined strange creatures running through jungles and swimming in seas.

We now know that those ideas about Venus were wrong. But we can still appreciate the fascinating world that Venus really is.

The surface of Venus in a photo taken using radar waves

FUN FACTS About MERCURY & VENUS

★ In March 1974, the NASA space **probe** Mariner 10 flew past Mercury, becoming the first probe to study two planets. Mariner had flown past Venus the month before.

★ Mercury is so close to the sun that, from the surface of Mercury, the sun would appear two to three times larger and about seven times brighter than it does from the surface of Earth.

★ Even though Mercury is very hot, there may be frozen water inside **craters** at Mercury's north and south poles. The floors of these craters are always in the shade, so it never gets hot enough there to melt the ice.

★ NASA studies of Venus's high temperatures and its atmosphere of **carbon dioxide** are helping researchers learn more about the global warming that many scientists believe is happening on Earth.

★ On June 8, 2004, Venus passed directly between Earth and the sun, appearing through telescopes as a black dot against the sun's surface. This will happen next in 2012—then after that, not until 2117.

★ Many craters on Mercury are named after such famous artists, musicians, and authors, as Beethoven, Shakespeare, and Homer.

Glossary

argon A chemical element.

astronomer A scientist who studies stars and planets.

atmosphere The mass of gases that surrounds a planet.

axis In planets, the imaginary line on which the planet seems to turn, or rotate. (The axis of Earth is an imaginary line through the North Pole and the South Pole.)

carbon dioxide A compound formed of carbon and oxygen.

core The center part of the inside of a planet.

crater A bowl-shaped depression on the surface of a moon or planet.

crust The solid, outer layer of a planet.

day The time it takes a planet to rotate (spin) once around its axis and come back to the same position in relation to the sun.

density The amount of matter in a given space.

diameter The distance of a straight line through the middle of a circle or a thing shaped like a ball.

elliptical Having the shape of an ellipse, which is like an oval or flattened circle.

equator An imaginary circle around the middle of a planet.

gas giant Any of four planets—Jupiter, Saturn, Uranus, and Neptune—made up mostly of gas and liquid.

gravity The effect of a force of attraction that acts between all objects because of their mass (that is, the amount of matter the objects have).

helium The second most abundant chemical element in the universe.

hydrogen The most abundant chemical element in the universe.

iron A metallic chemical element.

magnetic field The space around a magnet or magnetized object within which its power of attraction works.

mantle The area of a planet between the crust and the core.

mass The amount of matter a thing contains.

meteorite A mass of stone or metal from outer space that has reached the surface of a planet without burning up in that planet's atmosphere.

mineral An inorganic (nonliving) substance made up of crystals.

moon A smaller body that orbits a planet.

nitrogen A nonmetallic chemical element.

orbit The path that a smaller body takes around a larger body, for instance, the path that a planet takes around the sun.

oxygen A nonmetallic chemical element.

phase The shape of the moon or of a planet as it is seen at a particular time.

planet A large, round body in space that orbits a star. A planet must have sufficient gravitational pull to clear other objects from the area of its orbit.

pressure The force caused by the weight of a planet's atmosphere as it presses down on the layers below it.

probe An unpiloted device sent to explore space. Most probes send data (information) from space.

sodium A metallic chemical element.

solar system A group of bodies in space made up of a star and the planets and other objects orbiting around that star.

sulfuric acid A colorless, dense, oily liquid that destroys or eats away at materials with which it comes into contact.

vacuum Space that contains no matter.

year The time it takes a planet to complete one orbit around the sun.

Index

For more information about Mercury and Venus, try these resources:

The Near Planets, by Robin Kerrod, Raintree, 2002

Mercury:

Exploring Mercury: The Iron Planet, by Robert G. Strom and Ann L. Sprague, Springer, 2003

Mercury, by Seymour Simon, Sagebrush, 1999

Venus:

Venus, by Seymour Simon, Sagebrush, 1999

Venus: Magellan Explores Our Twin Planet, by Franklyn M. Branley, HarperCollins, 1994

Mercury:

http://messenger.jhuapl.edu/

http://nssdc.gsfc.nasa.gov/planetary/planets/mercurypage.html

Venus:

http://nssdc.gsfc.nasa.gov/planetary/planets/venuspage.html

http://www.nineplanets.org/venus.html